ACKNOWLEDGEMENTS

Words cannot express how excited I am to share this book with the world. God gave me a message: "When a Man Catches on Fire!" I shared that message with the men at a special service and what God did in that service was amazing! Now, I have been mandated to share it with the nations.

Let me say thanks to my loving wife, Liane. Thanks honey for your constant nudging and encouragement. God used you to pull this out of me and I love you for being the vessel that He used to bring me to the place where I needed to be in order to complete this venture. Love you Beautiful! Together we have this ministry.

To my wonderful children, Brandon, Jazz and Lei; what a blessing you are in my life! You are wonderful and dad loves you. I am just as proud of you as you are of me.

To the Galilee Baptist Church of Newark NJ, thank you all for your prayers and support. God has used you in such a special way to shape what He has in store for us. I tell you often and I tell you again I LOVE YOU! To the Men of

MAN ON FIRE

Valor, you are such a blessing to your pastor. You are truly Men on Fire!

To the First CRC in Crown Point Indiana, this book was written in part for our "Man of Fire" Prayer Breakfast. May God bless you and the women that He used to bring us together in prayer and this book to fruition!

To those who took part in editing I love you and thank you!

To Almighty God, it is only because of You that any of this is possible. Thank You for choosing to use me out of all that You could have used. I am humbled and will make every effort to make You proud of me. Thank You for trusting me with this assignment. Now bless it so that everyone who reads it will hear Your voice and apprehend the urgency of the call. Pour Your anointing out so that every man would surrender to Your Spirit and become "A MAN ON FIRE!"

Pastor Zan

MAN ON FIRE

INTRODUCTION

Psalm 8:4-5 "What is man, that thou are mindful of him? And the son of man that thou visitest him? For thou hast made him a little lower than the angels and hast crowned him with glory and honor." (KJV)

Man has a specific place in the heart and mind of God. As God was creating the world, He merely spoke and everything came to be. He said let the earth bring forth and every living creature that lives on this earth appeared. He spoke to the air and birds filled the atmosphere. We understand that all things were created by Him. Without Him nothing was made. His words have creative power. However, He did not use words to create man, He used His hands. He looked at what He had made and declared it was good. But when He got to man, He declared that man should be made in *"Our"* image. So, He scooped down and made man a body. When He breathed into man, he came alive with purpose. We were created to give Him praise and be in fellowship with Him. Not just with our mouth but with our lives as well. In Psalm 8, David asks a question. He wanted to know what was so important about man that God would care about him and visit him. He made angels and created the world. But he wondered what was so special about man that God has crowned him

MAN ON FIRE

with glory and honor. David respected and stood in awe of the splendor of God. In addition, he was equally amazed to know how concerned God was with the well-being of man. Well, what's the concern? Why *does* He give special attention to man? God pays so much attention to man because we are created in *His* image. There is not another species on earth that was created in God's image. Man bears the image and carries the breath of God. In other words, God has an investment in man. According to Paul, *"We have this treasure in earthen vessel..."* (II Corinthians 4:7). Since God has made an investment in us, then He has an expectation for us. He doesn't invest without having an expectation. The expectation that God has for man is that man will carry the good news of the gospel and live the gospel that he carries.

I must admit that from my observation, man is having a hard time carrying out the expectation of God. Many men find themselves too busy with being a husband, father and provider. So the mandate to be a Word carrier has fallen by the wayside because other things have demanded our attention.

Before I really delve into this book I need to share why it is so important that we as men regain our focus and

MAN ON FIRE

answer the call of God. I have had the privilege of speaking with numerous young people on a number of levels. From the classrooms, church workshops to community outreach programs and even juvenile detention centers. Unfortunately, the dialogues are the same wherever I go. It doesn't matter the color, race or nationality. The same problems plague the rich and the poor. The black and the white children are singing the same tune. "Where is my dad?" The question hits home when I take into account that a lot of these cries are coming from Christian homes. Men and churches from all walks of life have failed to realize that the need for the father figure is so vital to the success of our next generation. It can be summed up in the words of one of my students. I will call him Ricky. One day, while I gave one of my abstinence lessons, Ricky said to me and my partner teacher, "Thank you for that valuable information. I appreciate what you all have imparted and I will apply it to my life." Then he dropped his head and tears rolled down as he said, "But it should have been my father telling me this." Ricky NEVER knew his father and found that he is now longing for the one person who could have altered the course of his destiny with just one word. At that very moment I understood the importance of men in the lives of children. I further

MAN ON FIRE

understood that it is the Christian man who will not only impart direction but he also has the distinct task of imparting the truth of God. Direction without truth still yields chaos. While I believe that we often make choices that will have results that we would rather not face, I also know that if the foundation is not correctly laid then even more dire consequences will be the result.

Just as Ricky is aching for the guidance of his natural father, spiritually speaking our wives, children, churches and the world are crying out for the guidance of a man that is on fire for God. As Ricky has made known, those that are counting on us to lead the way can receive the message from someone else but they would much rather receive it from the one that God has put in their lives to deliver it to them. Yes they can follow God on their own because each relationship with God is personal. The point here is that we have left them to fend for themselves and hope for the best. But when a man deliberately and intentionally leads the way, then the spiritual success of those that follow will increase. The premise of this book is that every man who reads it would have his passion kindled so that he can sense the urgency of the call and be able to answer. My prayer is every woman that reads it will first pray for EVERY male in her life and then put this book in his hands so that he

MAN ON FIRE

can become steadfast in his faith and understand the power and authority that God expects every male to walk in. Are you willing to answer the call? May God speak to your heart? May you yield your total self to Him so that you can be a **_Man on Fire!_**

TABLE OF CONTENTS

Chapter 1 ~ Pass It On

Chapter 2 ~ Lay Down your Idols
(Chase the Lover of Your Soul)

Chapter 3 ~ The New Man

Chapter 4 ~ Man of Prayer

Chapter 5 ~ Men on Fire

MAN ON FIRE

CHAPTER 1: PASS IT ON

As I read of the events that took place in the early church, I noticed that there is a definite disconnect from what early encounters look like and what we experience today. In the early church the power of God was the main focus and not an afterthought. It appears that the church of today is missing something. While we have our new edifices, it appears that we lack the fire and passion of the early church. How beautiful our churches are with the lovely cushioned pews, central air conditioners, TV screens so that everyone can follow and participate in the worship. Our awesome praise dancers and praise teams are extraordinary but, in some churches they do very little to spark transformation on a regular basis. So something is yet missing. So, I must submit to you that rather than have gorgeous buildings where He is seldom invited, God desires to have a church that is full of fire. As I read the works of John Calvin, Martin Luther, Smith Wigglesworth, and read of the miracles wrought through A.A. Allen, Charles Finney and visited such great services of R.W. Shambach; I understand how God desires to use men. I have heard how Bishop Charles Mason, founder of the Church of God in Christ, was a praying man. He

MAN ON FIRE

was arrested during the time of segregation when prejudice was at its all-time high and in a southern state no less. The testimonies are recorded that as they had him locked in jail, he began to pray. As he prayed a cloud formed over the jail. Because this cloud formation was such a great phenomenon, the sheriff of the prejudiced county demanded that they free Bishop Mason because he feared what would happen if they harmed him. The moment they freed him the cloud disappeared. I marvel at how God protects what He has invested in. Without these great men (and there are many others that I could name) the world would not have been as effected as it is today. These great men caused great change. I believe that I have caught the heartbeat of God when I say that there is a greater desire on the heart of God than just having a church on fire. I believe that the greater desire of God is that men everywhere catch on fire. When men catch on fire and lead the way then the churches would have an unquenchable fire. I am speaking here of the kind of fire that causes us to fall in love with Him and not be ashamed. This fire also mandates that in order to stay kindled, we must remain in the presence of God. This concept was difficult for me to comprehend as a male, because as I reflect on my life, I can honestly say that I saw very few males that were on fire for God in the

MAN ON FIRE

church. The men that were seemingly on fire were often ridiculed by other men and became the object of scorn. So much so that others literally went to them and asked them to stop praising. Others who professed to have the fire often lived a double life. They lived one way at church and another way outside of the sacred walls of the sanctuary. You see, having the fire of God goes beyond the sanctuary. It spills over into regular everyday living and transforms your life! Even with your flaws you desire to become everything that God desires you to be. So, there was and continues to be a shortage of men that are really on fire for God. The question is haunting and will not go away because we hide under the cover or put our face under a pillow! Where is the army of men that will catch and spread the fire?

It is with this thought in mind that I feel compelled to write to men from every nation and denomination, of every color, race and creed! We as men must seek after the fire of God. Please understand that I am not disregarding the role of women in the body of Christ. Let me give you your props before I go any further. You have been outstanding as nurturers and have been instrumental in building the kingdom through preaching, teaching and wherever else your gifts and the Spirit have taken you. That cannot be argued. It is not my intent

MAN ON FIRE

here to minimize the role that women have played. Despite what men have been arguing down through the years the evidence is clear; God uses women in spite of the miniscule thinking of man. Male and females each have their place and roles. We need each other. Our success and growth depends on each other. However, there are certain things that genders can only glean from their gender. I am arguing that we have lost a generation of young men because they have allowed other things to kindle their passion. This is NOT because women have not done their job. It is because we, as men, have not shown and exhibited the fire of God. This is really not difficult to understand. The lack of spiritual leadership has had such a powerful effect. So much so that we have become comfortable with being spiritually blind and walking in darkness. We have become so content with our lack of spiritual sight, that when a man who desires more than just a Sunday morning fling with God raises up, he is often looked at as a fanatic. The call is and has always been to pass on what God has given. But, it is rather difficult to pass on what you don't have. The reason we can't pass anything on is because we have not positioned ourselves to receive from God.

It doesn't matter what church I go to, I see the same thing. The churches are full of women that have caught

MAN ON FIRE

the fire and passion of God while the men tend to be oblivious to the move of the spirit. Most men act like God has only poured His spirit on women and men are not supposed to be excited about the presence and power of God. The contrary is true. God desires that all of us show gratitude for what He has done and continues to do. Are there any reasons that so few men have caught this fire? Yes there are! Let me give you a few reasons that in MY opinion, we as men have missed the fire. First of all, from my observation I have noticed that most men are satisfied with merely coming to church and being in the building. Being in the building, for most is equated with being in a good Christian relationship. The importance of why we really come has not been realized. So to say open up your heart and let Jesus in is incomprehensible. The thought of going deeper never crosses our mind. In our minds we say, "I am here and you should be satisfied with the fact that I am here". Most are satisfied with spending some part of a Sunday and sending money rather than really getting into the presence of God! Unfortunately, the lack of desire for God has been passed on to the next generation. What we are witnessing now is a generation that has no respect or tolerance for God, let alone the fire of God. Whether it is intentional or not, the image

MAN ON FIRE

that we have passed down is that God should be a small part of our lives (when we can squeeze Him in) and not BE our lives.

Another reason that we have not caught on fire is that we have settled for the mechanics of religion. One thing that we must remember is that being in relationship with God should never be mechanical. In order to have a real heartfelt experience, this relationship must have its genesis in our heart. The ramifications of our actions have been detrimental even beyond what we can see. Since we, as men, have not passed on the notion of making God a priority, our next generation has made other things a priority. Oh I know that some of you may be saying that I lead devotions and pray at dinner in my home. Yes, those are the mechanics of Christianity! You are applauded for that. However, that is just the beginning. Realize that you have more to offer than just the mechanics and rituals of religion. Let me offer a scripture that I hope puts this point into perspective for us and shows us just how poignant this point is.

In Matthew 7:21-23 Jesus says,

"Knowing the correct password—saying 'Master, Master,' for instance— isn't going to get you anywhere with me. What is required is serious obedience—doing

MAN ON FIRE

> *what my Father wills. I can see it now—at the Final Judgment thousands strutting up to me and saying, 'Master, we preached the Message, we bashed the demons, our God-sponsored projects had everyone talking.' And do you know what I am going to say? 'You missed the boat."* (The Message)

While I love The Message translation of this verse, please allow me to paraphrase it if I can because I want to keep us in the proper vein. "Knowing how to do all of the mechanics of religion isn't going to get you anywhere with me. What I require is that you love me and serve me with a deep passion and not out of obligation but allow love to be your motivator. Yes, you can do many wonderful things **for** me but I'd rather you be connected **to** Me!" The King James Version says in verse 23, "depart from me I never knew you." The word "knew" here can be translated to *"intimate".* So He only knows those that are in intimate relationship with Him, not those who go through the mechanics of religion. Now the question is, "have you passed on the fire and passion?" We cannot be satisfied with mere mechanics because it does not please Him. We must go deeper so that it gets embedded in our hearts or else everything that we do is mere vanity. Most men have been in an empty mechanical relationship with God that has led

MAN ON FIRE

them to desire more. While they desire more, they don't know how to get it. What's even worse is they will lose their desire for more because all they have ever known about God is this mechanical side. Sadly, they resolve in their heart that if this is all there is to God, then I am good just like I am. Because just like faith without works is dead; works without faith will kill you as well.

As an educator and a pastor, I have learned that some people will learn from the words that I speak. Most, however, will learn by what they see me live. For many years now my sons have watched me fix their mother's plate after I cook dinner. They have watched me serve my wife, then my daughter and then I will fix and serve their plates. I noticed that when they serve our plates they emulate what they have seen. Without saying that they should serve the women first and make sure they are taken care of, they do it automatically. What are you saying Pastor Zan? People need a visual of what real passion for God looks like. Please hear the urgency in what I am saying. We need to pass on something that is not merely from what is scripted or mechanical. We must set a standard that will last through the ions of time. We must model it and live it in front of our children so that our children will pass it on to their children and their children will pass it on to their children and to their children. It has to be something that is visual so they can learn how to put it into practice. Without fail we must pass on the fire and passion. They will catch more from watching how you live it than from your teaching. Teaching provides the lesson and mechanics but being an example shows us how to apply what we have been taught. The greatest legacy that we can leave for our families is that of really knowing how to love God. It is imperative that they learn from **US** what it really means to be Christians that are on fire. I will reiterate again, ***it is more effective for people to see how much we love Jesus than hear how much we love Him!*** An important note about passing on what we have learned is that we must be genuine in what we do. People will only glean from those whom they can trust. So our passion must be real.

The question that challenges us still remains. **"WHAT ARE YOU PASSING ON?"** Remember, we as men are the catalyst for change. The call in the spirit is so urgent that we must pass on what the spirit of the Lord has put into us. Just look at the world today. If men of God who are filled with His power do not pass along the power of God, we will face another generation that goes through this life on spiritual cruise control and never engage in a true relationship with God. Without being in a true,

MAN ON FIRE

passionate relationship we are headed for a spiritual shipwreck. I ask again, **_WHAT ARE YOU PASSING ON?_**

MAN ON FIRE

CHAPTER 2: Lay Down Your Idols (Chase the Lover of Your Soul)

Exodus 20:3 "Thou shalt have no other gods before me". (KJV)

God as we know Him is an infinite, supreme being. He has no origin, yet He always existed. He was before genesis and the alpha. He started the beginning. He will surpass revelation and still have power after the omega. To try to describe Him using human vernacular is really a travesty. To try to describe this infinite God using finite terms is really an injustice. Some of the things that I have heard about God through the years are, "He is awesome", "He is great", and "Magnificent" just to site a few. I cannot forget to include the ever popular call and response phrase that swept through the church. The leader would say "God is good" and the audience responds, "All the time". The leader continues, "And all the time" the audience concludes "God is good." Though all of these phrases represent our attempt to describe our indescribable God it really doesn't convey all of who He is. I stand in awe of Him. God should be the object of our affection. We commit and pledge our allegiance to

MAN ON FIRE

demonstrate our love for Him. No matter how we choose to describe Him, we have the same responsibility. That responsibility is to embrace Him with our whole hearts. *Mark 12:29-31* says:

> *"And Jesus answered him, the first of all the commandments is, Hear, O Israel; the Lord our God is one Lord: And thou shalt love the Lord thy God with all thy heart, and with all thy soul, and with all thy mind, and with all thy strength: this is the first commandment. And the second is like, namely this, Thou shalt love thy neighbor as thyself. There is none other commandment greater than these."*

The place where God desires to be is on the throne of our hearts. He has prescribed the way that He wants to be loved. He wants to be loved with all our hearts, with all our souls and with all our strength. If we don't love Him as He prescribes, we will miss the passion of the relationship and be unfulfilled. When you feel unfulfilled you will begin to seek out other venues for fulfillment. When we chase after something and allow it to consume us, it becomes our God. So then another question must be asked my brothers. What are you chasing? It can be the God that we described earlier as being great or it could be a god of this world. When God created us He purposely left a void on the inside of us. There is a

MAN ON FIRE

longing in us for something more. When we don't allow God to fill that void, we seek other things to fill it. What we fill it with in lieu of Him only provides temporary satisfaction. Jesus addressed this issue with the Samaritan woman. She was seeking instant self-gratification. Jesus was trying to get her to understand the importance of worshipping the Father in spirit and in truth and all she was concerned with is this was her ancestor's mountain and keeping the rituals. He told the woman at that well in John 4:13-14,

> *"Everyone who drinks this water will get thirsty again and again. Anyone who drinks the water I give will never thirst—not ever. The water I give will be an artesian spring within, gushing fountains of endless life."* (The Message)

More plainly put, we keep trying to satisfy our thirst with things that satisfy for the moment. However, we find ourselves thirsty again. The principle that we should take from this is that spiritual thirst cannot be quenched with natural sustenance. Since God put the void in us, He is the only one that can fill it up.

MAN ON FIRE

WHO OR WHAT ARE YOU THIRSTING FOR?

Let me ask a question; "What drives you?" What is the one thing in life that ALWAYS gets your attention? What's the one thing that you must do no matter what comes up? All of us have something that drives us. These things are not always negative. It could also possibly be things that are good as well. Things such as desiring to be the best husband or father could be included among the list. Working to the best of your ability and being punctual so that you can be promoted could be another motivator. Exercising so that you can be in optimum health is another area of focus. In most cases, these motivators are admirable. I mean it's not like those who are driven by the body's demand to feed a crack addiction. Neither is it like nerves that have been trained to become tranquil when nicotine or alcohol is introduced into the body. Those are the obvious. But what if even the good things that drive us, come into conflict with God? We must be careful not to allow superficial things drive us and become our point of focus. Most men today are still searching for what their heart loves. We have settled for empty relationships and have been crippled with fear. Fear has gripped us so

MAN ON FIRE

much that even what God has for us eludes us. We then spend our time in search of things that will fill the longing in our heart and quench our thirst. Some will become so intoxicated with instant gratification until they will ignore pending dangers.

The Song of Solomon chapter 3:2 puts it this way, *"I will rise now, and go about the city in the streets, and in the broad ways I will seek him whom my soul loveth: I sought him, but I found him not."* This love for her drove him to go look for her. It's okay to seek something like that as long as it is God. But again I ask, what if what we look for like that is NOT God? Remember God has to fill the void. Make no mistake; **WE WILL SEEK TO HAVE THAT VOID FILLED!** Some try to fill it with drugs, alcohol or sex. Some try to fill it with playing or watching sports, working long hours or partying. There is no shame about that because we are ALL guilty of not making sound choices. For some, risking it all for someone they loved was the norm. We have been disobedient for the sake of love. We have been defiant. We ignored what our parents taught us for the sake of fitting in. We have even endangered our health and well-being just to satisfy the urge within us. Knowing what we know about the effects of alcohol, we went against our better judgment and yielded to the temptation. We all have had things in our

MAN ON FIRE

lives that we would do anything to have or keep. Though this may sound extreme, there are those in prison that have even killed for what they wanted. The possibility of spending time in prison was overshadowed by the need to feed the thing that was driving them. I have called for the saints to be honest when it comes to sin. Most of the time when people refer to life before Christ, they often refer to it as being miserable. The truth that we must admit is most people did NOT lead a miserable life of sin. We loved the sin that we were committing. Sin often feels good to the flesh so we like it. It's the consequences that we don't want to face. So let me ask this question, what if the very thing that we love drives a wedge between us and the real lover of our soul? What if what we loved is standing in the way of making our calling and election sure? What if the very thing that you loved so dear offends the One that you need to be complete and whole? What would you do? Which one would you choose; faith or familiarity?

Let's go back to the scripture so that we can face reality. Whatever you have allowed to thrill you will be what you fall in love with and in turn become your lover and that's what you begin to search for. If you love alcohol you will search for your next buzz. Drug addicts search for the next high. Married or not we search for the next

MAN ON FIRE

sexual gratification. Again, like the woman at the well we come back again. Why do we repeatedly return to the same thing that has the capability to not only lead to our natural destruction but also our spiritual demise? It is because we have NOT changed lovers! When we change lovers we will get a new perspective. When God becomes the one that our soul loves we will lay down our idols. We can and will lay them down because we will understand that NOTHING compares to Him! No drug can take you higher and no lover will ever love you better.

Why change lovers? Okay let's examine why this change is a necessity in your life. Up until the time that you have what I like to call a *"God Encounter",* your life will continue to be on a vicious cycle. Most of us would spend our lives going up and down in and out. This seemed to be our destiny. Included in this cycle is a ton of questions that needed to be answered as well. (Keep in mind that these questions are born out of a warped understanding of who God really is.) Is being a sports fan bad? Is dating wrong? Is having a love for grilling food and playing sports not pleasing to God? What about going to the beach? I love music. Does my music offend Him? I have been asked these questions numerous times. I must answer them in light of the grace of God. In perspective, these things are not wrong in God's eyes. He wants us to enjoy life to the fullest! They can, however, offend God when we love them more than we love Him. We must seek to bring our lives to balance. There are many people who started out genuinely loving God and didn't mind working for Him. Somehow their intentions and focus became perverted. Now instead of their motives being pure, they are simply motivated by greed and selfish gain. Consequently, they love working for God more than they love Him. Never put the work of ministry ahead of ministering to Him. Don't let the act of worship replace true worship. Don't love to sing His praises more than you love Him. Never love to lift your hands in worship more than you love to worship Him. Never love being in His sanctuary more than you love being in His presence. Never love the blessing more than you love the One who provides the blessing! He is our focus and the center of everything. Making God the focal point of our existence may not be popular in this day and age but it is definitely a sign of maturity. There comes a time that we as men must grow up. I Corinthians 13:11 says *"When I was a child, I spake as a child, I understood as a child, I thought as a child: but when I became a man, I put away childish things."* (KJV) When we were little boys there were certain

MAN ON FIRE

allowances that were afforded to us. It was understood that we would make mistakes as we were growing. After several lessons and mistakes, consequences were given if we kept making the same mistakes. We had consequences from our parents, in particular because they loved us and not to exploit short comings. Even now, there are some things that we will not engage in because those consequences still ring in our mind. However, we must admit that we are better for it. That's the power of love. One thing that I must impart here is that I have discovered that real Love causes one to mature. Without maturity real love does not exist. My brothers I know chronologically we are of age but mentally some of us are still so very immature. I say this because most are still waiting for a parent to discipline us. We are grown now and must discipline ourselves. We are no longer that little kid with an abundance of allowances and pardons for our disobedience. The expectation as a man is that we make the proper decisions that will cause our lives to prosper. When are we finally going to tell ourselves that I have done enough partying? When are we finally going to grow up and stop using women as a pawn in our sexual games? To view them merely as conquests or another notch in our belt is immature. Running from our responsibilities is

MAN ON FIRE

immature. Real men don't always do everything right. We face and admit our mistakes. We handle what we need to handle with pride. We don't blame our short comings on the grey goose got me feeling loose as suggested in a popular song. We terminate our selfish attitudes and now consider how our actions will affect those around us. Enough is enough! I say that because like Ricky in the introduction the cries of many youth demand that we lay down our idols and embrace maturity. There are certain sects in the world that perpetuate ignorance and immaturity. They use vulgar language and sexual innuendos and images to keep the minds of many in bondage. Men of God, we cannot let those images be the only image that is seen. If those are the only images that are visible, then that will become what their souls love. God still cries out, "Have no other god before Me." The need to change lovers and lay down idol gods is crucial and becomes more critical every day. Without hesitation or reservation we must begin to lift up the name of Jesus so that our sons, daughters, wives, co-workers and neighbors would be drawn to Him. Lay down your idols and grab Him with both hands. It could make the difference in the life of someone that is following you. "Who is following me" you may ask. "I never asked anyone to follow me." No

MAN ON FIRE

you didn't. But, here is the crazy thing about life. In everything we do and say somebody has purposed that they want to pattern themselves after you. There is a boy watching how you treat your wife. There is a person gleaning from your work ethics. There is a fatherless son taking notes on how to treat his son. There is a fatherless daughter observing you as you interact with your daughter and is mentally and emotionally etching in her heart how a real man treats his wife and consequently how a daughter should be treated. Most of all, there is a sinner learning how to approach your God through you and learning what it means to love and live for Him with joy and passion. Are you showing them your idols or exhibiting the power of your God? Are you showing them the mechanics of religion or the power of an intimate relationship with God? The challenge is for us to love Him so much that we mature in Him. We can't do it holding on to idols that block our maturity. Let go of your idols and embrace God so that others who are watching you would desire to embrace Him as well. Make Him the lover of your soul so that you will chase only after Him.

CHAPTER 3: *THE NEW MAN*

II Corinthians 5:17 *"Therefore if any man be in Christ, he is a new creature: old things are passed away; behold all things are become new." (KJV)*

All of us have done things that we are not too proud of. We have not made all the right choices. We have fallen short several, well let's be honest, hundreds of times. We have spent years trying to improve ourselves to become what the world says a "real" man is. So we have become obsessed with doing manly things. Watching sports, going fishing, golfing, hanging out with the guys and discussing our struggles with life has become a point of focus. Taking care of our wives and children and providing for them has become a priority. From the outside looking in, it appears that we have it all together. But no one really understands how we feel when we feel like we have failed on any of these levels. Most of us have failed in some aspect. We have let not only God and our families down, we have failed ourselves. Let me take this moment to call you from

MAN ON FIRE

under condemnation and into freedom. You can be new in Christ.

Let's refer to the first man that is mentioned in scripture, Adam. After God created all of the animals, He said "Let us make man in our image." Prior to creating man, God declared that it was good. It was good but it was lacking something. Nothing bore His image. Having the image of God, God gave Adam the authority to name all the animals. God walked with Adam so much that He agreed with whatever he named them. Adam said 'let's call that one with a long neck and patches a giraffe." God said "I like that". "Let's call the one with the long teeth and mane a lion." God said "well done." And so it went. Adam must have been the pride of God's creation. How proud God must have been! Adam found favor in His sight because God walked with him and two cannot walk together unless they agree. (Amos 3:3) Brothers, when is the last time that you can say God walked with you? I am not talking about His omnipresence being with you all the time. At this point, what I am speaking of, is knowing beyond any shadow of doubt that He is walking with you because you feel His tangible presence. You are moved to make it known to those that will hear you, the only thing you want to do is please Him. We must know that walking with Him signifies that He trusts us with His

MAN ON FIRE

anointing and His presence. When was the last time He walked with you and you were so captivated by Him that it didn't matter what you were lacking; your goal was merely to spend time with Him? When was the last time you became so engrossed in His presence that whatever and whenever He asked of you yielded an immediate yes? When was the last time you walked with Him with blinders on so that you would not be distracted by the things in life and been comfortable just following Him? Here is another question. When was the last time God got excited about coming to visit you? When was the last time that being in your company brought God so much joy that He didn't want to leave? I believe that God was excited to visit with Adam for several reasons. First, Adam made God his life. He loved making God happy. He magnified God. Not once do we read where Adam complained about anything that God asked of him. Adam was so content to be serving God he did not even realize that he didn't have a female counterpart. It was God who said it is not good for man to be alone so He created and presented Eve to him. Up until this point, pleasing God made Adam happy. When was the last time that we can honestly say that pleasing God was so important that we didn't miss what we didn't have?

MAN ON FIRE

When you keep Him first, He supplies ALL of your needs according to His riches in glory.

The second reason that God was excited to visit with Adam is because Adam gave Him his undivided attention and got into His presence without rituals and traditions of men. This demonstrates how God originally desired to fellowship with man. Without being prompted by a worship leader, without the singing of a praise team, Adam acknowledged and basked in the presence of the Lord. He embraced it because He knew that being in the presence of the Lord is where he wanted to be. It was his refuge. It was his protection. It was his light and salvation. It was his strength. It was in the presence of the Lord that He lived, moved and had his being. Adam basked in the presence of the Lord and found the fullness of joy. He sat at the right hand of God and found pleasures forever more. Everything that Adam needed he found in the presence of the Lord. He was excited to be in the garden because it was beautiful and had everything he needed; but when he heard God walking in the garden and he realized that God was coming for a visit, his heart skipped an extra beat.

You know how the rest of the story goes. Man fell into disobedience. His innocence was lost. The way that God

MAN ON FIRE

interacted with him changed drastically. The purity of the relationship was lost. Please understand that Adam's fall affected the entire world. When we as men fall and refuse to get in and remain in our God-given position and walk in the authority of God, other things in life will also fall out of alignment. While there may be the appearance of external success, the root of the problem will continue to be spiritual and internal. The void is evident. While some make millions, they are addicted and overdosing on drugs. They abuse their wives and children. They live in the illusion of happiness yet thousands are committing suicide. Some, while not rich, live at the other end of the spectrum. They murder without regret. They don't value education so they disrupt class to hide the pain of the internal struggle. They can't seem to find their way. We may not all experience the same things that life has to offer. Though we may live in different neighborhoods and states and countries and have different ancestral heritage, here is what those illustrations confirm for me. It doesn't matter what your socio or economic status is. The one thing that I know to be true is, **"When your spiritual compass is off your life will harbor chaos."** Our world is full of people whose compass is off. They are leading people away from the centering power of the Holy

MAN ON FIRE

Spirit. The structure of the family is under attack and the world seems to be grabbing this attack with a heartfelt embrace while God is grappling with men trying to get us to take him seriously. Divorce is becoming the norm. The dysfunction between parents and children is brazen. We must realize that God is the core. When the core is shaken everything is thrown off balance. The good news is that God has provided a remedy. We have the cure in Jesus. He must become the core of our lives! Guess what? He enjoys being the center of our lives. He enjoys it so much that rather than destroy Adam, He forgave him for being disobedient. Adam wrapped himself in fig leaves to cover his nakedness. Sound familiar? Men do the same things today except we don't use fig leaves. To cover our hurt and shame and to enhance the idea that we can somehow escape the presence of the Lord, we drink, smoke, push loved ones away, become abusive, become introverted, selfish, self-reliant, arrogant, stubborn, develop self-destructive behavior, become unteachable and argumentative just to name a few. Do you think that you are the only one who has tried to get away from God? Listen to how David describes his attempt at trying to get away from God. Here is what Psalm 139:7-12 says,

MAN ON FIRE

"Is there any place I can go to avoid your Spirit?
To be out of your sight?
If I climb to the sky, you're there!
If I go underground, you're there!
If I flew on morning's wings
to the far western horizon,
You'd find me in a minute—
you're already there waiting!
Then I said to myself, "Oh, he even sees me in the dark!
At night I'm immersed in the light!"
It's a fact: darkness isn't dark to you;
night and day, darkness and light, they're all the same to you. (The Message)

Since we can't get away from His presence, we must let Him help us instead of denying Him complete access. We think that piling on the fig leaves will cover the pain. Therefore we spend our lives covered in leaves. But what we fail to realize is that underneath all of the fig leaves is a man that is still wounded and hurting. Fig leaves do not heal hurt they merely cover the nakedness. Fig leaves represent a temporary fix that can only take care of the superficial outward manifestation of an inward condition. The fact that Adam and Eve were naked was the least of their problems. The bigger problem was that they severed ties with a holy God. Because of their sin He could no longer just come and chill. He could not allow His holiness to be tainted with the unrighteousness of man. So He says "I'm going to take your temporary fix and give you a permanent solution, my Son Jesus." So God goes and sheds the blood of animals and dresses Adam and Eve in the skins. The fact that the animals had been slaughtered suggest that God purged and forgiven them for their sin because without the shedding of blood there would be remission of sin (Hebrews 9:21-23). He clothed them in the skins of the animal that was sacrificed to signify that salvation can only be found in what has been provided and ordained by God. Man had to be robed in the skin of the sacrificed animal. The Bible declares that the wages of sin is death but the gift of God is eternal life. (Roman 6:23).The fall of man shifted the relationship between God and His creation. God made a point of dressing Adam and Eve in the skin of the animals and it was a poignant one. Because the fall of man created an entrance for sin, God was now in the position that He could not look at sin and not kill or punish the perpetrator. So every time He saw them in their animal clothes it reminded Him something already died so that they could live and further punishment was not

MAN ON FIRE

necessary. Jesus says the same things about us to the Father every time we fall short of the glory of God. When the undeniable sentence of our sin should be death Jesus exclaims to the Father, "They have accepted the work of the cross. I died in their place. Although I knew no sin, I became sin so they could become your righteousness." Though we may have to face certain consequences for our actions, when God looks at the cross He sees our sins on Jesus and when He looks at us standing around the cross He sees His righteousness. He sees us covered in the blood of His dear Son. Right now I know that I am not the only one that is grateful for Jesus dying in my place. He forgives ALL of our sins. The only way he could forgive them all is that He had to die for them all. No sin was left out. All sin is subject to the blood of Jesus. No demon can overpower it! The blood still has miraculous power. Thank you, Jesus, for taking our place and giving us your righteousness.

Christ is longing for that same pure intimate relationship from us that He had with Adam. Although we have fallen so many times God has provided a way that we could return to Him, Jesus. Most of us may feel like our lives are beyond repair. The real truth is that we are never beyond repair in the sight of God. We must seek the wisdom of God. Only God's wisdom will satisfy our

MAN ON FIRE

spiritual thirst and hunger. I bought a car recently and it came with a warranty. The warranty was valid as long as I went to an authorized dealership. Even if it was a simple matter of changing the oil, going to an unauthorized dealer would nullify the warranty. So when something happened to my truck, I had to call John. I had to take my truck to where John directed me. Anything contrary to John's instructions nullified the terms of the contract. It releases him from any further financial obligations and the burden now falls on me. I know that some of you have many questions regarding your destiny and what the plans of God are for your life. But the reason that you have not gotten any resolution concerning your situation is that you go to unauthorized dealers and therefore breech your contract with God. Since He is our core center, He is the only one that orders our steps with the compass of His word. When in doubt you must refer to the owner's manual. In this case, I am referring to the word of God.

I need to speak a personal word to you right now. There are many of you who are reading this who want a fresh start in your life. Let me help pull you up. There is no pit so deep that His grace can't go deeper. Wherever you find yourself, you must trust that God has a plan for your life and it does not include you failing. It does, however,

MAN ON FIRE

include your victory. There is one thing that is your sole responsibility in this deal; you must get in Christ. And again, I am NOT speaking of a mundane religion and the meaningless rituals that come along with it. I am talking about the fire and the passion of being in relationship with Him. Whatever it is we do for Him it should be motivated purely by love. Let's see if I can paint a picture so that we can see this point clearly. As corny and unmasculine as it may sound, I'm going to take a stab at revealing part of my love for my wife in this analogy. There are times when I want to show my wife how much I really love her. So, I'll do something just because. Like fix an outstanding dinner and serve her plate. I may send a text that says, "I love you beautiful". There were times that I would buy flowers and a card and say "Just because it's Wednesday!" I would show up at her job with lunch and flowers and snacks so she wouldn't get hungry during the course of the day. At night I rub her feet and hair. Sometimes I just sit and watch her. I do this because I love her, not because I am expecting something in return. When I treat her like that the actions are reciprocated. Vivian, one of my sisters from Trinity Christian College celebrated a birthday. She was so overwhelmed with what her husband, Herb, gave her. Because he loved her so much he held nothing back and

MAN ON FIRE

spared no expenses. Vivian was so excited about what he had given her that she took pictures and posted them all over Facebook for the whole world to see. So it is with God. He wants us to love Him so much until we don't care what anyone thinks or says. When we pour our love on Him He crowns us with glory and honor for the world to see and nations then call us blessed. We have it wrong. We are NOT emasculated because we love Him and are not ashamed to proclaim this to the world. No matter how much you have messed up, He has the power to steer your life back to the route that He has intended. How does this happen? II Corinthians 5:16-17:

"Because of this decision we don't evaluate people by what they have or how they look. We looked at the Messiah that way once and got it all wrong, as you know. We certainly don't look at him that way anymore. Now we look inside, and what we see is that anyone united with the Messiah gets a fresh start, is created new. The old life is gone; a new life burgeons!" **(The Message)**

It is alright to forgive yourself for your mess ups because God has made forgiveness available to everyone that will receive it. You can be a new man in Christ. My

MAN ON FIRE

brother, come and experience the joy of being in the presence of God. You really aren't living until you get in Christ. In Christ all things are new and your past is gone. Let's stop right there. How can my past be gone when I can vividly remember getting drunk and doing some of the things that I did? I remember the hurt that was inflicted on me and I, in turn hurt others. Some of you are still tormented by the guilt of the past. Guilt therefore cripples your future. You can't be a good father, husband, communicator, provider or worker because of the damage that was done to you until you get in Christ and allow Him to wash you completely. Once you are in Him you will be able to look beyond the shame of your mistakes and embrace the fact that God was getting glory even in the rough times. Brother, get in Christ and begin again. Your wife has been praying for you. She deserves a godly man and your children deserve a godly father. Your church deserves a man who is passionate about God. The world is waiting for you. The question for you is "Do you want to continue wearing the fig leaves that you have sewn together and continue avoiding the presence of God?" The alternative is that you can come into His presence as messed up as you may be and allow Him to dress you in what He has

MAN ON FIRE

sacrificed. The fig leaves or the animal skin, the choice is yours.

# CHAPTER 4: *MAN OF PRAYER*

As I reflect on my childhood, I remember being entrenched with knowing the importance of prayer. It was the initial genesis to growing in faith. Believing that there is a God had to be accompanied with being taught that we had to talk to this invisible God in sincerity. Having us pray to a God that we could not see was a lesson of faith. Hebrews 11:1 ***"Faith is the substance of things hoped for, the evidence of things not seen."***(King James Version) As a child, I can remember very vividly being taught to say my prayers before bed. Kneeling and repeating after my mom was a nightly ritual. She led me in prayer until I was confident enough to say it on my own. I am 100% sure that all of us were taught to pray one of two prayers if not both. One is loved throughout the world in countless cultures and nationalities. That is the "Our Father" prayer. The second is just as popular and loved no less. It began something like this "Now I lay me down to sleep….." I know that you can finish the rest. And after praying, we would snuggle up and rest soundly through the night. Bedtime prayer as child had been so ingrained in us that we felt funny if we didn't do it. Even if we were in situations that we couldn't say it

MAN ON FIRE

loud, we knelt and quietly prayed. I need to stop here and say that as we matured chronologically that in some cases, our desire to communicate with God did not. So prayer is still left as a bedtime ritual even after all these years. If we are going to mature in Christ, prayer cannot be left as merely as a bedtime habit. This concept is essential because this habit of overlooking the power of prayer is indicative to the world situation. Most believers have not gotten that sense that it is high time for believers to go before the throne of God beyond the bedtime ritual. As I look back at my spiritual upbringing, I am thankful to have been introduced to Christ and the weightiness of talking to Him. While I appreciate the introduction to prayer that was afforded to me, I am also painfully attentive to the reality in my life. The truth is that as time progressed and I got older, I lost the fire and desire to pray. In fact, even the urgency of that bedtime prayer diminished as well. I am sure that this scenario is not solely my testimony. For some it went even further. Some even lost the desire to even spend time with Him at all. For the sake of not wanting to rebel against what we were taught, if we continued doing what we were taught although our hearts were not in it. We lost the innocence and sincerity and maintained a facade. If that is the case, then I must ask "What got in

MAN ON FIRE

the way?" Was it the kickball games? Was it the girls? Was it being able to hang out a little later? Was it going to the movies or sitting up late watching cable? Wait, I know. It was that while I was taught that God wanted to hear from me I was NEVER taught that **PRAYER IS VITAL TO THE GROWTH OF EVERY BELIEVER; WHEN PRAYER STOPS SO WILL YOUR GROWTH!** While I had built a strong foundation, I had not built maintenance into my life style. I often reflect on my life during those times. Upon self-examination; I see where my spiritual life had been stunted because of the lack of prayer. I see now that the enemy's plan is to keep us pre-occupied with stuff so we can't get our directions from God. I read something once on a bumper sticker that really blessed me and turned my heart back to prayer. It simply said **"Seven days without prayer makes one weak."** I was in church yet I was missing out on the best part of serving God, spending time with Him. Furthermore I knew that I didn't want to be a weak Christian so I knew that every chance I got I had to spend time with God.

DEVELOPING A PASSION FOR PRAYER

Many people often inquire about where my passion for God and prayer came from. So, I guess now would be the perfect time to share my heart and my experience.

MAN ON FIRE

When I finally understood that prayer would be the key to my success, I immediately gained a desire to pray more than just at bedtime and at church. It is essential that we recognize that deep relationships are not formed in the public view for examination. The formation of deep intimate relationships occurs in private without the analysis of an audience. What we see in public is a result of what has taken place in private. Relationship with God is not cultivated merely by an appearance at church. It is not heavily fostered by the occasional prayer. Unless they are void of common sense, morals and are unscrupulous, very few people get really intimate in the public's eye. Respected conception takes place in private otherwise it is labeled as unlawful conduct. Those who engage in such behavior can be arrested for indecent exposure and lewd acts. Developing a love for God may be ignited at a church service or reading a book or wherever God encounters you. However, that passion and growth is only maintained in private. I can truly say that at the onset, I didn't know what God wanted to do with my life. I just knew that He was calling me. I wanted to conceive His plan for my life. However I couldn't conceive it while I was directing the choir or being an usher. I had to remove and shed everything that had a remote

MAN ON FIRE

possibility of hindering what God wanted to do in my life. Another major breakthrough was unearthed as I began to delight myself in Him. I discovered that as much as I was enjoying being in the presence of God, like Adam, He was enjoying ME being in His presence as much as I was enjoying Him.

I was so blessed in my high school years to have come in contact with brothers who also had developed this kind of passion for prayer. Dave and Pedro are my Spanish friends who attended a Spanish Pentecostal church. So they were serious about seeking God. The second group of prayer partners that the Lord allowed me to share with, was Stan and Kervin. Occasionally, in this group we were blessed to have our beloved sister, Arlene. We would spend hours after school in prayer. We would pray in our cars and pray in our homes. We would even pray in our public school during gym. We would often shut in on the weekend. This consisted of fasting, praying around the clock at designated times, Bible study and admonishing one another in the Lord. When all of us got together what a blessing! People around us didn't understand our passion. We only knew that we wanted to conceive from God. The first suggestion that I will offer is this, in order to become a man of prayer you must surround yourself with people that recognize the power and importance of prayer. As miniscule as this may sound it is the yeast that will revolutionize your prayer life. I developed consistency and passion through accountability to the brothers. There was not one day that we were NOT stepping into the presence of God. We would never let each other make excuses or become lazy or ever approach God half-heartedly. We wanted to ensure each other's spiritual success. If there were issues we discussed them and encouraged one another so that we could approach God with a pure heart. We wanted to go before our God and we didn't want to approach Him in just any manner. We wanted to purify our hearts and minds so that nothing would impede us from His glory. The more we prayed, the more confident we became in the God that we were not only **talking to.** Even more importantly, an overwhelming confidence grew in the God that we were **talking about.** We had spent so much time with Him we developed sensitivity to His presence. We were actually living I John 5:14-15 which says:

> *"This is the confidence we have in approaching God: that if we ask anything according to his will, he hears us. And if we know that he hears us—whatever we ask—we know that we have what we asked of him."*
> **(NIV)**

MAN ON FIRE

Because of those prayers and heeding the spirit's call to come deeper in prayer, we saw the miraculous. All glory and honor to God for the great things He has done! We have seen blind eyes come open, tumors shrink, cancers dissolve, broken bones mend, and the list goes on. I have even seen God heal my god-daughter from HIV. We will never declare that we were perfect. We will always proclaim that we sought after the perfect God. In seeking after Him, He makes all things new and His grace covers a multitude of sin and puts us in right standing with Him. So I hope you understand that <u>*He is not looking for perfect people but rather He is looking for a people to perfect through His blood.*</u> It is through His blood that we have been made whole. Through consistent prayer, our faith grew by immeasurable leaps and bounds. The miracles that we experienced introduced us to another side of God. We learned that there was no distance in the power of God and that He could be everywhere at the same time and do whatever He wanted to because He is God. There were many ways that God proved Himself to us. This is why our foundation is now unshakeable. Please keep in mind that I am not bragging on myself. All glory and power belongs to God. I am bragging and boasting about the

MAN ON FIRE

power of the God I serve. He is the God of Abraham, Isaac, Jacob and Zan! And He's your God too!

PRAYER IS INTENTIONAL

Another aspect that I must include in this discussion of becoming men of prayer is an important one. I must point out that what we experienced did not haphazardly or accidentally occur. It was intentional. We had to desire to come closer than what could be experienced on a Sunday morning or during family devotions. Let me pause here because I want to be perfectly clear. God is **NOT** asking that we neglect our families. He is, however asking that we spend some quality time with Him. You see, we must fully understand that our families are not just asking for strong men. Your wife is not merely asking that you pay the bills and provide for the family. Your son is not merely asking that you be there for games and play ball with him. No, your daughter is not only asking that she be the apple of your eye. Your family is crying out for a godly man to lead the way. You can equip your children to be the most intelligent in their class. You can provide and make it so your family wants for nothing. But if you have not given them the spiritual direction that they are crying for everything that you have given them means nothing because it

MAN ON FIRE

won't stand in the last day. Our job as men is to usher our families into the presence of the Lord. They may not understand everything that you do or even like it. But when **you** become confident in following **God's leading,** your **family** will become confident in following **your lead.** They will follow you as you follow Christ. A family will submit to a man who has submitted to God. A praying man will become a godly man. The purpose and power of a praying man is found in James 5:16 "***Confess your faults one to another, and pray one for another, that ye may be healed. The effectual fervent prayer of a righteous <u>man</u> availeth much.***" (KJV) Here is how it reads in the Message including verses 17 and 18.

"Make this your common practice: Confess your sins to each other and pray for each other so that you can live together whole and healed. The prayer of a person living right with God is something powerful to be reckoned with. Elijah, for instance, human just like us, prayed hard that it wouldn't rain, and it didn't—not a drop for three and a half years. Then he prayed that it would rain, and it did. The showers came and everything started growing again."

A godly man has been entrusted with a power that only comes from God. God has endowed a praying man with purpose. A man that walks in his God given authority can turn his home toward God. In turning a home toward God, a neighborhood can be turned. In turning a neighborhood toward God, a city can be turned. The result of turning a city toward God is a state can be turned as well. When a state is turned, a country can be turned. In turning a country a nation can be turned. In turning a nation, the world will have to focus on Jesus and claim Him as Lord. This reveals the power of prayer. We have that authority. II Chronicles 7:14 gives the believer an assurance. It says, *"If my people, who are called by my name, will humble themselves and pray and seek my face and turn from their wicked ways, then I will hear from heaven, and I will forgive their sin and will heal their land." (NIV)* We must become persistent in our prayers and not become discouraged. Prayer is a weapon of a man on fire and we must not be afraid to use it.

COMMUNICATION IS CRUCIAL

Prayer requires that we communicate. While at Trinity Christian College, I took a communication class. I learned a lot from the instructor. One of the points that Mrs. Ward made that I have never forgotten is that

MAN ON FIRE

communication involves two roles; a sender of a message and a receiver of a message. In a conversation these roles are interchangeable. The person who says "Good Morning" is the sender of the message. They say it to someone who receives it. The roles now change. The person responds and sends the message "I am fine, and you?" The other person who initiated the conversation receives the message and may elect to send out another message. This could go on for hours while the parties go back and forth between the roles of sender and receiver of messages. Here is the point that I gleaned and applied to my life. It has become embedded especially in my prayer life. Most of us approach prayer as a monologue and not dialogue. We enter it by talking to God and sending Him messages. Here is the wonderful catch that most of us fail to apprehend. **<u>He wants to dialogue.</u>** He wants the opportunity to respond to our request. He wants to engage in interchangeable roles with us. When we send Him the message "Lord, I have lost my way." He wants to respond, "My word is a lamp unto your feet and light unto your path." When you send Him the message, "Lord, I feel weak and don't know if I can go on", it moves Him. He wants to respond, "He wants to respond to you, "My strength is made perfect in your weakness." When we fail to allow Him to

MAN ON FIRE

be the sender of a message we develop a lopsided relationship. The problem with a lopsided relationship is that someone always feels empty. In this case, it is God. When we won't allow Him to engage and answer our questions and comfort us, I believe that it hurts Him. Just think about the many times that you had the answer or a warning for someone but they failed to heed what you had to say because they thought that they could handle it on their own. You became frustrated and angry. You probably asked yourself, "Why won't they listen to me?" God says I am the Lord that "forgives all your sin, heals all your diseases and redeems your life from destruction." Then He asks, *"Why won't you let me do in your life what I have the power to do?"* When we fail to communicate with Him, we fail to know Him! Oh, He knows all there is to know about us but we know NOTHING about Him! How sad it must be for Him to be viewed solely as a sounding board and gift giver and not a friend. Greater love has no man than this that He would lay down His life for a friend. He has laid His life down so that He could elevate the nature of our relationship with Him from servant to friend. In most relationships with Him, He is our friend in theory but not in reality. If He were our real friend we would long to spend time with Him. We would desire

MAN ON FIRE

Him like David in Psalm 27:8 *"When thou saidst, Seek ye my face; my heart said unto thee, Thy face, LORD, will I seek."* (KJV) Nothing becomes more important to us than the presence of the Lord.

For some men, one the most difficult things for us to do is communicate effectively. One of the most common complaints that I hear from wives is, *"My husband doesn't communicate with me!"* Because of the level of difficulty that most men experience in this area and the level of commitment that is required, most of us will neglect to develop a formidable prayer life. We do pretty good with our family devotions and bedtime prayers, but when it comes to being a man of consistent prayer and having personal passionate prayer with God, most will fall short. **BUT IT DOESN'T HAVE TO BE THIS WAY!** Throughout this book I have been saying how important it is that we become passionate about our relationship with God. The key that is so vital to the kindling of that passion is prayer and time spent with the Master! There are many people from all walks of life that are reading this book. Some have had different experiences in the church. There are charismatic and non-charismatic believers that are reading these words. Here is the thing, the call for passion and prayer is for all to answer. You can't pray and not be moved to spark a revolution in your life. The question is, "Do you want change in your life?"

GOD'S OUTLINE FOR PRAYER

Prayer is so essential to your success as a believer that Jesus gave instructions on how to pray. He never intended for prayer to be reduced to a time where we merely submit a laundry list of things that we need Him to do. I mean you would not like it if every time your wife opened her mouth it was to tell you things that you were not doing and things that she didn't like about your appearance or your work around the house. Every once in a while you need her to compliment what you have done. So that we would capture the essence of prayer, He modeled it for us in Matthew 6. He also never intended for us to be stuck within the boundaries of praying the same prayer every day because that would become mundane and less heartfelt. According to verse 9-14:

> *"This, then, is how you should pray Our Father in heaven, hallowed be your name, your kingdom come, your will be done, on earth as it is in heaven. Give us today our daily bread. And forgive us our debts, as we*

also have forgiven our debtors. And lead us not into temptation, but deliver us from the evil one." (NIV)

I believe that this is a roadmap that serves two purposes. First it will cause us to enter into the presence of the Lord. Secondly, it provides us with insight to what God expects prayer to be. According to the outline, before we delve into prayer we should acknowledge who He is. He is our Father! After we acknowledge Him we must worship Him. Hallowed or holy is His name. Before we present our request, we praise and thank Him for what He has done but, we worship Him for who He is. Then after we spend time in worship and adoration, we move to asking for the will of God to be done. Please note that the kingdom of God is not heaven. It is God's way of doing things here on earth. It is the way God intended for the world to operate. According to the text, it is okay with God that we pray for daily bread. This means that we have the okay from God to pray for the things that are necessary for our daily survival and success. They can and should be brought before the throne. It is totally acceptable to God that we pray for wisdom and the means to live in this world. It is Him who gives us the power to get the wealth and have good success. However, let me say that there must be balance. There is divine order in prayer. Our self-

MAN ON FIRE

gratification is NOT at the top of the list; He is. The next step is forgiveness. Forgiveness is a vital part to enjoying prayer. There are several things that we need to understand about forgiveness. The first thing that we must understand is that in order to obtain forgiveness we must forgive. In that same scripture of Matthew 6:14-15, we find these words in The Message:

"In prayer there is a connection between what God does and what you do. You can't get forgiveness from God, for instance, without also forgiving others. If you refuse to do your part, you cut yourself off from God's part."

The King James Version says if we don't forgive then we can't be forgiven. If this is true then we must make a valiant effort not to harbor unforgiveness. This is NOT an option and our prayer success depends on it. So who do you need to forgive in order to receive the forgiveness of God? Is it your wife? Is it your children? Is it the boss? If you are harboring anger and bitterness then you hinder the move of God in your life. You can always tell when the spirit of anger is prevailing in a person. Because they are not living in obedience to God, they feel free to be sarcastic, facetious, put down, dismiss feelings, belittle, ridicule, avoid real issues and become vessels that spew hatred and hurtful words of

MAN ON FIRE

condemnation. Sometimes we don't realize that we spread our venom of hatred. It is not difficult to understand! If hatred is in you, then that is what will eventually come out; especially under pressure. You can conceal your words but your actions speak volumes of the internal affairs of your heart. The reason that it is so important to forgive is because there is no hatred in God. So hatred does not look like Him. Our goal for becoming a man of prayer is so that we bare His image in every area of our lives. You've got to forgive your parents for not understanding who you are and failing to bend you toward who God made you to be. You must forgive your dad for not being there for you. You must forgive your mom for being angry at your dad and taking out the hurt and resentment that she was feeling toward him on you. You must forgive that man that molested you. You have never been able to articulate it but part of you died and you have never been able to love completely because part of you has been taken away. So now you drink to mask the pain. You don't know how to relay this message to your wife so you treat her less than what she deserves to be treated. Notice now, that because you have not forgiven, it has infected your whole life. It is only when you forgive the person that hurt you and then forgive yourself that

MAN ON FIRE

God's forgiveness can be realized in your life. Some of you may be saying these examples are little farfetched. Let me assure you that it is more common than what most of us are ready to accept. That leads me to another principle point. As we become men of prayer we must also pray that God make us sensitive to the needs of our brothers. There is a reason why our brothers drink uncontrollably, get stoned out of their mind and take risk with their lives. Men of prayer don't sit in judgment or the seat of the scornful. After we become fervent prayer warriors, our mission becomes to bring others into the knowledge and power of our God. However, we can't effectively teach forgiveness if we haven't forgiven. Without forgiveness the last part of the model prayer which entails praying to be delivered, will be nullified. A person who won't forgive is already consumed with evil thoughts and evil intentions. Deliver us from evil will never occur without forgiveness. The Message states, ***"If you refuse to do your part, you cut yourself off from God's part."*** We must completely understand that if God is going to do His part then we must obey what He has commanded us to do.

MAN ON FIRE

A STATE OF EMERGENCY

As I survey the world and it's seemingly perilous irreversible state, I am gripped with a sense of how urgent it is that we become men of prayer who carry the fire of God. I am being summoned to further admit that God wants to move mightily among us but there is no passion on our part to come close to Him. Not only are there few witnesses but there are even fewer men of prayer. A lot of people want to blame President Bush while others will point the finger at President Obama for the state of our economy and nation's condition. Well I want to suggest to you that we must look a little deeper. The state of our union is not simply the fate of a president. Included in this fate is a lack of praying men. Not only is the economy in state of emergency, but our world's spiritual state is in peril as well. He is not looking for us to band with other religions in prayer. Those of other religions cannot call on Him whom they have believed or served. We cannot operate with diluted power. It is God's pure power or no power at all. He is looking for men who believe in the power of His name to unite in prayer. I will give this last illustration before I close this chapter. I went to Iowa to do a Bible camp. Although New Jersey is the Garden State and has corn

MAN ON FIRE

fields, I had never seen so much corn in all of my life. It was there that Randy imparted knowledge to me concerning corn. The first thing that he shared with me was that corn had genders. There are male corn and female corn. For every four rows of female corn, there is one row of male corn. First of all, the fact that there are genders blew me away. Then to learn that without the male corn, the corn could not reproduce fascinated me even more. Where there is no male reproduction is nonexistent. This principle holds true even in the spiritual realm. Why do you think king Herod ordered the death of all the male children when he was trying to kill Mary and Joseph's new born? The enemy understood that where there are no males there is also no potential for sustained life. Spiritually speaking, the enemy is trying to destroy the male. If he can stop men from praying then the possibility of having posterity that knows the power of prayer drastically diminishes. We cannot allow another generation to exist without knowing the power of God. They know the Wii, play stations, Farmville, Facebook, cyber bullying, text and sexting, but they don't know God. This is a state of emergency. In a state of emergency the army or some branch of military is called in to help. Well, God is calling in the army of powerful praying men who will stand

MAN ON FIRE

erect and pour on this generation the power and love of Christ. We have sons and daughters who are losing their way. Other entities are luring them away from the faith that has been embedded in them. They are killing themselves and one another. Mothers are crying over them and now it has become imperative that we as men step up and begin to cover them in prayer. Men are to always pray and not faint. It's not open for debate or discussion. The bottom line is this, the only hope a miraculous turn and hope of a godly win is if men catch the fire and would pray. Lives can be transformed if we would pray in power. Stop making excuses as to why we can't do it. Lives are at stake. The Spirit of the Lord is calling. He is rising up an army and you must respond. Become a man of faith. Become a man of prayer so that you can turn and transform a life for the kingdom of God. Don't delay. I hope your heart is sensing the urgency. Like the female corn cannot reproduce without the male, there will be no future of the church unless godly men step up and begin to pray and pour the spirit of prayer and faithfulness on this next generation. While godly women are holding their position, they are praying for godly men to pour on them to ensure the posterity of the church. They can't do it without us. Spiritually and naturally it is impossible. This is a state of emergency!

CHAPTER 5: MEN ON FIRE

From the last chapter I sincerely hope that you heard the pressing call of the spirit. You can make a difference. It is so critical that we become men on fire for God that for some of you, He is stirring your passion even now as you read. There is no need to worry about how it will happen. Just give Him a yes and make strides toward keeping the vow. That is your sole responsibility. Since the directive is coming from the Spirit of God, then it is His responsibility to provide what we need to be successful when we answer the call. Fire is part of the essence of who God is. He spoke to Moses through fire that did not consume a bush. (Exodus 3) Since He is the Good Shepherd and always leads His people, in typical God fashion, by fire He leads the children out of Egypt. (Exodus 13:21-22) On Mt. Carmel at the showdown between the prophets of Baal and Elijah, by fire He proves that He alone is God. (1 Kings 18:30-40) Jeremiah says that it's like fire shut up in my bones. (Jeremiah 20:9 and Lamentations 1:13) So it is clear that the presence of fire in scripture alludes to the presence of the spirit of

MAN ON FIRE

God. The New Testament continues with this concept as John announces in Matthew 3:11:

"I indeed baptize you with water unto repentance. But he that cometh after me is mightier than I, whose shoes I am not worthy to bear: he shall baptize you with the Holy Ghost, and with fire."

It is imperative that we note that in other verses in the gospels that talk about Jesus' baptism, namely Mark 1:8 and John 1:33, the word fire is omitted. Only Holy Ghost (In King James Version) appears. This simply means that when the Holy Spirit comes fire will accompany Him. This is confirmed in Acts 2. When the Holy Ghost fell not only was there a mighty rushing wind that came in the room, but cloven tongues of fire also sat on each of them. It symbolizes that the Holy Spirit now occupied the vessel. Let me show you the difference between a man who is on fire verses a man who is not. Let's look at Peter as a perfect example. Let's look at his life pre and post Pentecost. Before Pentecost occurred Peter had a job as a fisherman. He had a temper and would often use vulgar language. So Jesus appears to Him and says come follow me and I will make you fisher's of men. There are two points I want to make here. The first is that not even God can use a man who is idle. In order for

MAN ON FIRE

God to use him there has to be something that captivates his heart and mind and causes him to move toward God and answer the call. Anything that captivates your attention will cause you to take action. God wants to captivate you so much that you will move out of your idleness and get in hot pursuit of the one who has your heart. Let me be clear, I am NOT necessarily talking about merely having a physical job because we can do physical activity and still be idle in our mind. If we are not engaged in mental activity, our minds will have a difficult time when it comes to doing daily tasks. God wants a heart and a mind that will not squawk at the opportunity to engage in spiritual tasks such as prayer and fasting. A person who is idle in deed and thoughts will never seize the moment. They will always declare that they will catch it the next time it comes around. They become slothful and disobedient. Please remember that delayed obedience is still disobedience. I wonder how we would react if God was delayed in waking us up every morning. We must begin to come close to Him without delay and hesitation.

MAN ON FIRE

CALLING OF THE IMPERFECT

The second point that I must raise about Peter's calling is that God didn't call the perfect. Peter was not perfect but he was perfect for the task that Jesus needed him to do. Please remember that He calls those that are perfect for what He needs to get done not those who are necessarily perfect according to man's standards. How many times did Peter miss the mark? His thinking was off and he didn't see everything the way that Jesus saw them. God doesn't deal with us based on where we are. He sees us for everything that we can be. Notice, even in Peter's imperfection, Jesus took him into the sacred circle with James and John. I sure hope you hear God speaking to you. I know you think that you have too many things that are wrong with you. Because of those things, you think that God can't possibly want you. My brother let me assure you that the nothing could be further from the truth. Just as He knew of Peter's imperfections when He called him, He knows yours as well. Why does He call those who are not perfect? I am convinced that He calls us just to show off His grace and mercy. He proves to the entire world that He is God. Here is what He does. He takes a life that has been torn apart and good for nothing except to be trodden under

MAN ON FIRE

the foot of men and puts it back together again. He proves to the nations that just because people have given up on you, doesn't mean that He has given up. So let me encourage you. In spite of your past He wants to pour His fire on you so that you may have a future and an expected end. No matter what you have done, He knows that you are better than what you are right now. So He won't give up on you until He brings out the best in you. Let Him pour His fire on you.

Peter had done some miracles, but it was only at the command of God because he had not really been transformed in his thinking. He just operated at the command of the Lord and obedience to God's command. The command of the Lord and obedience to that call is what generates the power. The fact that he along with the other disciples and the seventy that were sent out came back and started rejoicing that demons were subject unto them denotes that they were immature. Jesus told them not to rejoice because they had cast out demons, but rather rejoice that their name was written in the Lamb's book of life. (Luke 10:17-20) Men, misplaced praise is not praise at all. It's simply tinkling cymbals and sounding brass. We should always praise God for what He has done and allowed us to do. It is not by our might but it really is the power of God.

MAN ON FIRE

Transformed people are mature enough to know that if anything good happens it's because of Jesus. Many of us can look at our lives and see where plenty of good things have happened even when we weren't good. The enemy would have us look at what we have and become content right there. You can have all of the money in the world and still be broke. Look at the house you live in. The job you work on. Look at the health of children. Most of you will say that all those are intact. So it becomes easy to take on the attitude of things are going so well for me I can be content. We have sunken into such a lull of contentment that we don't realize that God has a longing to set us on fire. Like those seventy, we rejoice over what we have and have done and don't see the greater reason for praise. The truth is we can't appreciate the greater reason of praise because we refuse to possess the fire of God. When we possess the fire of God we would not need things to trigger praise. We have the fire and the fire is continual. Since the fire is continual the praise should be continual as well. Once, I was at a convention and the theme was "Powered Up". So I just wrote a quick verse and chorus to a song and taught it to the band. That evening we taught it to the kids. It was the night that Christian Rock met urban gospel. What a blast the band and I had watching the

MAN ON FIRE

kids clap and leap for joy and leading them in the style of worship which for some was their first experience. One of the leaders said that it was vain repetition. My thought was "Are you kidding me? Were you so preoccupied with counting how many times we repeated some words that you couldn't enjoy the presence of God? You have just missed the outpouring of joy!" Let me just state for the record that praise is never vain if it is from the heart. I ask you my brothers, "How many times is too much to tell your wife that you love her?" I mean do we reach a certain quota and then never say it again? Or, are you like me and feel like you can't say it enough? Well if I feel that way about my wife and she never gets tired of hearing it, how much more does God need to hear it? Better yet, how much more does He desire to hear it? The more we pour our love on Him the less we will pour our love on other things that won't please Him. So all of the days of my life I will praise Him because He is worthy. Praise is so intertwined in every fiber of my being that if I fail to praise Him I will cease to exist. He is my reason for living and my reason for living keeps me praising. Because of the fire of God, my praise is perpetual.

MAN ON FIRE

TAKE ON HIS ATTRIBUTES

Another vital point that we must mention is that while Peter walked with Jesus, he had failed to take on the attributes of God. In the Garden of Gethsemane where Judas brought the soldiers to capture Jesus we see that Peter's proclivity to act first and think later comes through once again. As they begin to take Jesus away Peter pulls out his sword and cuts the guard's ear. Some may conclude that Peter was justified because he was protecting Jesus. However, we must realize to protect Jesus using worldly methods is no defense at all. We must pick up His attributes and act like Him if we are going to represent Him. How disappointed Jesus must have felt to know that Peter still had not caught the intent of His mission after three years. Much like His disappointment when Thomas had not realized that Jesus was the way, the truth and the life. Jesus said I have been with you for a long time now and you still haven't caught on. If you have seen Me then you have seen the Father. My brothers please don't make this same mistake. We are in church doing all the right things and still don't know the purpose and heart of the one that we say we are working for. We miss God. If we never intend to catch His heartbeat then why are we

MAN ON FIRE

doing what we are doing? This is why we are still empty after we do most of the stuff that we do in His name. Not only have we not caught His heartbeat, we are living in a surreal frame of mind. The reality of serving Him has not gripped us. You know how to function well in your position in the church. You know how to rally the troops at your church. You have good hospitality skills. You are happy that your wife is active in the church, **BUT** the joy of serving eludes you. You will be like Thomas and Peter. You will work for Him and be in His presence and still not know Him or understand His purpose. You cannot clearly and effectively work to the best of your ability without passion and fire. A person who works without passion is a person that spends the day waiting for dismissal time to arrive. The joy of working is replaced with complaining and discouragement. They punch out early and have not given an honest day's work. But a person who understands the heart and purpose of the job will be upbeat, jovial, and optimistic and will motivate others to do and be the same. Up until this point Peter has not understood what Jesus was really after, him! Brothers if He could ever get us, then He can get our talent and gift. Many of us are trying to present our talent but we won't present us. It is us that He is really after.

SEEK TRUE RELATIONSHIP

As we further study the life of Peter before Pentecost, the next point that we must examine is that he denied Jesus. Matthew 26:69-74 says:

> *"All this time, Peter was sitting out in the courtyard. One servant girl came up to him and said, "You were with Jesus the Galilean." In front of everybody there, he denied it. "I don't know what you're talking about." As he moved over toward the gate, someone else said to the people there, "This man was with Jesus the Nazarene." Again he denied it, salting his denial with an oath: "I swear, I never laid eyes on the man." Shortly after that, some bystanders approached Peter. "You've got to be one of them. Your accent gives you away." Then he got really nervous and swore. "I don't know the man!" Just then a rooster crowed. Peter remembered what Jesus had said: "Before the rooster crows, you will deny me three times." He went out and cried and cried and cried."*

While Peter had done miracles, he also failed to secure true relationship. Without the fire of God you will deny Him. Before the day of Pentecost, the disciples were operating out of sheer obedience to the word of God.

MAN ON FIRE

They had not yet received the fire. They had spent so much time with Jesus until they developed His accent. This means there was something very distinctive about them. Rather than wearing it as a badge of honor to be recognized as a disciple without carrying a Bible or wearing a gold cross around his neck, Peter feared for his life and denied Jesus. Having head knowledge without fire and heart conviction will lead to your denying Him as well. How do we deny Him? When we choose to spend time becoming intoxicated rather than being engulfed with His presence, we deny Him. When there is an opportunity to share His love and we don't because of fear, we deny Him. When we fail to let our buddies know that we are Christians and partake of their in godless actions, we deny Him. When there is no fire of the Lord present you will resort back to your old habits. Peter denied Christ but when the young lady said your accent is the same as Jesus' he resorted to cursing the way that he used to. The next thing he did was weep. He wept because he had denied the one person who had shown him unconditional love. He failed at the one thing that he was required to do and that was let the world know that he loved Jesus. The truth came out. When it was all said and done, he had been around Jesus but had not developed a level of intimacy where he would rather

MAN ON FIRE

with Him die than live without Him. He could no longer rejoice about the devils being subject to him now. He forgot about being so overwhelmed in the presence of the Lord that he never wanted to leave. He forgot about the feeding of the five thousand and the healing of his mother-in-law. Brothers we can spend so much time basking in the blessings that God has given us that we forget that every blessing comes from God. So we spend time protecting the things that He has blessed us with rather than nourishing our relationship with Him. Then something in us begins to weep because our spirit longs to connect to God and He is always longing to connect with us. We often deny the two an opportunity of conception so that something wonderful can be birthed in our lives. As Peter and the rest of the disciples did at the time of the crucifixion, we go into seclusion; emotionally, mentally and spiritually. In typical God fashion, He finds them where they were at their lowest point. Guess how He does it. He walks right through the wall, their false sense of security. If God is going to pour the fire on you, you must let Him in the walls that we have allowed to shelter our hurt and mask our pain. We are grown men hurting because we haven't dealt with our little boy issues. We feel safe behind those walls yet we are lonely and miserable at the same time. Because

MAN ON FIRE

we have been let down and hurt so many times, we find it difficult to really stand up for Him. Hence, we deny Him. Here's the thing, when we deny Him we deny His power and without Him our course is set for destruction. Can't you see that He has come through your walls to point you to the only possible resolution? FIRE! Come from behind these walls, let your guard down and get to the place where He can pour His fire on you.

GET OUT OF YOUR COMFORT ZONE

When Jesus walked through those walls He told them to come out of this seclusion and to meet Him in Galilee so they could receive the promise of the Father. In order to receive what God has for us, we must leave our comfort zones. We must leave the place where the abnormal has become normal. If the disciples had remained there, the fire would never have fallen on them. Here was another chance for them to answer the call and operate in the truth of why they were really called. To leave the room meant that they would be putting their lives in danger. Armed with the desire to continue what Jesus had begun in them, they left their place of safety in pursuit of what God had for them. They sacrificed their lives to come into true relationship with God. I need you to remember

MAN ON FIRE

that God has created something greater for you than what you have created for yourself behind these walls. You must be willing to sacrifice self-pride, fear of perception and ridicule to get the fire.

Let's skip forward and discuss the results of leaving the comfort zone. So far we have looked at the life of Peter pre-fire. Now let's look at him post-fire. When Pentecost had come, the Holy Spirit filled each of the one hundred twenty that were in the upper room and fire sat on each of them. They all began to speak in tongues as the Spirit gave utterance. Because of the Pentecost celebration, many people from different regions and nations were gathered in Jerusalem. They heard these one hundred and twenty people speaking in their language. This was a strange phenomenon because those who were speaking had never studied the language yet they were fluent in what they were speaking. Without stuttering and stammering, the Cretes heard their language. The Parthians heard their language. The danger here is to stay focused on the phenomenon and miss the bigger picture. The bigger picture is that this was the jump start of the church and it was birthed in fire. If it took fire to get it started then it will take fire to keep it going. Let's look at how it transformed Peter in particular.

MAN ON FIRE

There were a group of people standing around who mocked what they heard. They went on to accuse the one hundred and twenty of being drunk. Peter who was now filled with fire stood up and began to preach. The fire burned up his message of denial and gave him a message of salvation. The fire burned his unstable thinking and transformed his mind. Now he could be changed. He had no regard for his life. Remember to come out of hiding meant that he would surely be put to death. Peter became driven to have his life hid in Christ. He was determined to have his life flow with the power of the God that He had once denied. No longer would he deny Him, he was ready now to die for Him. Until the fire fell on him, Peter had no direction. He thought he was living just to be around Jesus because that's what brought him joy. But receiving the fire afforded him the opportunity of having life in Christ. This is poignant because some of us are around Christ but not in Him. The fire allows you to come close and experience His heart and get to know His mind. That's not where it stops. You WILL SHARE WITH OTHERS WHEN YOU ACQUIRE THE FIRE. A man on fire is a dangerous man because he is unstoppable and destroys things in his path. When we catch on fire we begin to touch and destroy the things around us that are not of God. We

MAN ON FIRE

don't tolerate sin and injustice. When we catch on fire we become infectious. We are contagious and everything in our path catches fire. It starts at home with our wives. Then it goes to our children, and so on. When we come into the sanctuary the fire spills onto the pew and touches the person that we sit next to. When we lead worship there is something distinct that happens. People will leave saying what an awesome time of worship. A man on fire will not just lead worship, he leads us to the presence of God. This fire is unquenchable. Troubles can't extinguish it. People can't stifle it. Satan's schemes cannot douse it. Understand that everything that God gives is eternal. For example the breath that He gave us is eternal. The Holy Spirit is eternal. To this list we must include the fire that he gives is eternal as well. He has never intended to be in a powerless relationship with us. He wants to turn the heat up until we are moved to live in holiness, boldness and become the inspired passionate leaders that He has called us to be.

An attribute of a man on fire is that he is not ashamed to own his God. As I was preparing for church one Sunday, I heard part of a message from TD Jakes that I want to share. It had to do with celebrating our wives. It is imperative that we understand that they love to be

MAN ON FIRE

recognized. But it is not so much of giving the flowers; it is where you give the flowers. You can give a dozen roses at home and she will be thankful. Have those same flowers sent to her job and she will be overwhelmed. God is thankful that you celebrate Him in your private devotions, but He becomes overwhelmed when you love Him enough to celebrate Him in public. Even God celebrated Jesus in the public at the baptism. A dove descended from heaven and a voice declared "This is my son in whom I am well pleased." In essence He was saying you have my approval. What a celebration! God celebrated His Son publically because of what He was getting ready to endure on behalf of sinners. We, in turn, ought to celebrate Him publically for what was divinely accomplished. When we praise Him openly we are saying to Him and the world, You have my thanks. A man on fire is not thankful with just mere words; his life reflects his gratitude in every area.

I understand that for some of you, this is a reminder and a call for you to rekindle the passion that you once had. For others, it is a mighty stretch. You have never expressed anything about God without reading it from a script that someone else wrote. Let me say no one can tell your story like **YOU** can. When you catch on fire no script is needed to share your love. You have friends

MAN ON FIRE

who like you are good natured, good providers, good husbands and excellent fathers. What is going to set you apart is the fire of God. You may have problems. You may be in between jobs. The thing that will get you through every situation is the fire of God. The fire of God will motivate you to keep moving and not become stuck in the mire of depression and self-pity. The question is "Are you ready to be a man on fire?" Are you really ready to love Him so deeply that it hurts when you can't be in His presence? Sometimes you will cry. Sometimes you will lift your hands. The mention of His name will send chills down your spine. Are you ready to lead you wife and your children not just to church, but lead them into His presence? God is calling you. Your family is praying that God would set you on fire. Your pastor and the men of your church are waiting for you to ignite so they can explode as well. God is tired of men who are just going through the motions. He wants a man that He can celebrate openly so He can pour His glory on him. Receive the anointing and the power. Focus and real relationship awaits those who will take the challenge. Be a man of God; a man on fire!

www.ingramcontent.com/pod-product-compliance
Lightning Source LLC
Chambersburg PA
CBHW060418050426
42449CB00009B/2010